Narcissism

A Mindful Guide To Entering The Narcissist's Mind And Repairing Gas Lighting Damage

(The Most Effective Manipulation Method Used By Narcissists)

Zackary Jensen

TABLE OF CONTENT

What's Potential And What's Not 1

Do You Want To Stay Or Should You Leave? 9

Methods You Can Employ To End That Toxic Relationship 24

The Secret Narcissist 37

How To Deal With A Narcissist 47

Trauma And Narcissistic Bonding 64

How To Spot A Narcissistic Mother Right Away 74

Techniques Of Command And Control 89

Disorder Of Narcissistic Behavior 101

Solutions For Narcissistic Personality Disorder .. 106

How To Handle Narcissists And Prevent Their Negative Effects On You 122

Don't Try To Change Narcissists While Dealing With Them. 142

What's Potential And What's Not

Narcissists never take responsibility!

They seldom, if ever, are prepared to accept responsibility for whatever they do that is improper since they see themselves as either flawless or worthless. They see acknowledging they are incorrect and taking responsibility or blame as admitting they are flawed and unworthy. If they do take responsibility, their self-esteem is destroyed, and their difficulties with self-hatred surface. Additionally, they believe that you will despise them due of their "flaws," which makes them feel worse.

Do you recall the fight about who would clean the kitchen before the movie? Your narcissistic partner is now in a better frame of mind, so let's go on. They want to embrace you and say good morning, but you won't let them. You told your friend that the disagreement had spoiled the evening. They turn the tables on you and accuse you of making them wait by choosing to tidy up the kitchen rather than watching the movie first. The debate then starts over again with these wildly divergent points of view.

Narcissists never apologize - As you now know, narcissists refuse to take responsibility since it would be too embarrassing for them to do so. Having said that, even if they are aware of their error, they are unlikely to apologize. Expect no apologies, at least not spoken ones.

Offering sweet offerings, such as taking you out to your preferred restaurant or purchasing a gift and surprise you, is a narcissist's idea of an apology. Accept the reparative gesture and give up your desire for an apology if you want peace and the relationship to recover from the disagreement.

Choose which fights to fight - You should learn to let go of unintentional, insignificant insults. If you repeatedly complain to your narcissistic partner about their insults and wounded emotions, the relationship will soon deteriorate and you two will be at odds all the time.

Even if talking instead of arguing would be so much simpler, arguments should break out when you are the target of major insults that go beyond certain lines that you would protect by leaving and terminating the relationship.

Be ready to quit and leave the relationship if your narcissist disrespects the limits you have established and refuses to accept responsibility.

Keep in mind that if you don't correct your narcissist and allow them to get away with it, they will say and do anything they want.

Narcissists don't want to talk about or process past conflicts - If you decide you want to talk about your most recent conflict, what went wrong, and how to handle it better in the future, your narcissist will refuse to even bring it up. They believe you are pointing out their errors and just reminding them of their inappropriate conduct, rather than really attempting to resolve your issues as a pair.

Use the pronoun "we" when referring to your shared previous conduct in order to attempt to be successful in finding a better way to disagree. Using the pronoun "you" merely fuels the flames of a narcissistic mind process that implies you are against them and are singling out their behavior.

Defend the Limits You Have Chosen to Establish

The limits of other individuals are never noticed by or respected by narcissists. If you don't make the decision to be clear and establish the parameters of what constitutes bad narcissistic behavior and draw the line between what they say and do that is tolerable and what is intolerable, your narcissist will have no qualms about saying and doing whatever they please without giving you or your feelings a second thought.

Narcissists have no qualms about publicly criticizing your ideas (if they vary from their beliefs), your family, your appearance, your choice in music and movies, or anything else you can think of. In an argument, a lot of their comments and jabs will be low blows. Then, later, they will behave as if there was never ever a fight and nothing occurred. They will say horrible and terrible things.

Some narcissists don't mind making embarrassing public spectacles - To certain narcissists, public situations that may render you humiliated are nothing. This may range from leaving a crowded restaurant because someone is taking too long to take your order to noisily shouting, fighting, and overtalking you as you attempt to get a word in edgewise.

A narcissist will repeatedly behave in any of these ways if they experience it once. They react to the impression that their sense of self-worth is being violated in this manner.

You must select where to put your limits and where to draw the line at this point. If they engage in whatever actions, in your opinion, are the most disagreeable, you must make it plain that their conduct is unacceptable. If they don't respect you and your limits, be ready to terminate the relationship.

Your relationship with a narcissist should stop at this point because physical violence may develop from verbal abuse. It would be a good idea to put an end to your narcissistic partner's verbal abuse from the start, unless you like getting hit and abused and have no limits about it.

If you don't create boundaries and declare that physical abuse is a boundary for which there is no justification and a relationship deal breaker, it will escalate very fast from a stinging arm hold or squeeze.

Relationships with narcissists are never simple, particularly ones with significant others. However, if you educate yourself on narcissist behavior and how they think and behave, it will go much more smoothly if you decide to continue in the relationship.

Set limits for yourself and steadfastly uphold them. Draw the line with a narcissist, and you should be able to withstand the difficulties that come with dating someone with NPD.

Do You Want To Stay Or Should You Leave?

Take a moment right now to consider every narcissistic relationship you have ever encountered. Write down beneath each of them all the justifications for your decision to remain with them as well as all the ways that connection has helped you develop. Justify your continued involvement in such relationships. And most importantly, look closely at who you are now compared to who you were.

Ask yourself whether you are acting from your most true self if you have decided to remain in the narcissistic relationship. I want to know whether you are being the most true version of yourself because when a narcissist meets with a genuine and honest person, something intriguing occurs. In today's culture, the term "authenticity" is overused, but what does it really mean? Authenticity: What is it? Those that accept and embrace who they are are considered to be authentic. They don't take things personally as a result. They don't make situations about them.

People who have had their fair share of pain or difficulties are those who are authentic. These are the individuals who persevere in spite of the challenges they have faced. They allow themselves to be exposed without worrying about how others will react or if they would judge them for it. When you are thus real, you become self-assured and give less weight to other people's views because you respect your own.

Therefore, it seems as if you will approach the narcissist with knowledge while you are being your real self. You won't be duped by manipulative and egotistical behaviors. The narcissist feels very frustrated by the fact that you are not falling into any of their traps. Narcissists find genuine individuals uncomfortable to be around. Because you know how to react to the narcissist's grandiosity—you listen, recognize, then move on to the next subject—authenticity will assist you avoid totally enjoying the narcissist's conceit.

Sadly, many who remain in narcissistic relationships lose their sense of themselves. And if you choose to remain with a narcissist, it is something you should consider. Think on who you want to be rather than what you are becoming or who you will become after years of experiencing narcissistic abuse. Ask yourself whether you are willing to adopt the right perspective to handle a narcissistic relationship in a manner that won't have an emotional or mental impact on you.

Even while entering into such a relationship might be intimidating, if you decide to remain, you must develop self-love and self-acceptance. The narcissist won't always have faith. They won't vouch for you or accept your account of events. They'll act in the other way. You must thus believe in yourself and develop self-control. Your knowledge must be sufficient given that you are aware of the situation's reality. You must have a strong attitude and positive self-talk.

It's not always necessary to provide an explanation or make a case for oneself. Speak your truth to reconfirm yourself, not for your partner. Be open and sincere at all times because when you do, the narcissist's game is over. To be real, you must let go of what other people think and say. You must be kind to yourself. You must learn to recognize when to remove yourself from a situation in order to be aloof from the narcissist and not tolerating or enabling their harmful practices. With elegance and courtesy, retrieve. You will achieve this by taking away the narcissist's control over you.

Once you can recognize manipulation and know how to react to it, no one can control you. You must develop to a point of self-actualization where you are congruent with yourself and are aware of who you are. Will the narcissist have any impact on you? Yes. You will experience life's difficulties and be let down by those you trust because you are a human. So, keep your identity and aspirations in mind while you negotiate your narcissistic relationship. Help yourself so that the narcissist's abuse won't alter your true nature.

Work on yourself, on your self-development, and learn to be gracious in your interactions. You make the decision to put in the effort necessary to repair yourself and remain loyal to who you are. To become resistive, be genuine and less concerned with what the narcissist says. The greatest way to develop resistance is to believe in and cherish who we are. We give narcissists too much credit, which is why they have such a strong grip on us. Their ideas and views are valued almost excessively by us.

Protect your heart and intellect above anything else. You spend most of your time in your thinking. You need to constantly cleanse your mind of the poisonous effects of narcissistic retribution. To be in good physical, mental, emotional, and spiritual health. Numerous opportunities will arise throughout life. Trials will increase your fortitude and toughness. When you recognize the behaviors and learn how to react to them, exposure to narcissists will make you intelligent.

We are in a self-development period, which is wonderful, but we also need to learn how to develop spiritually and care for our mental health. Do you live with or date a narcissist? If so, it's time to take steps to improve your mental health. You are sufficient and valued. It's time to contemplate and consider your true identity. You will grow more resistive to the narcissist the farther along the journey you go toward learning to appreciate yourself.

Start with self-discovery if you lack self-confidence and feel uneasy. You can't respect yourself or expect respect because of all the anxieties you are dealing with. Learn to pay attention to your gut instinct and intuition. Take action if anything does not seem right. Be wise in your response and think before you speak.

You are only living this right now. Every day you awaken is a day less of life, not a day more that you get. What will you do with your time as you move toward the day when your time on this planet ends? Will you keep putting up with emotional abuse because you are codependent and unable to recognize your own worth? Will you take responsibility for your actions, start to heal, and have the confidence to fight for the life you want?

Your period of pleasure and happiness must start now because the clock is ticking. You are the one who will save yourself from your present predicament; you are your own hero. Take power back, and don't just live to survive—thrive! You deserve a ton of happiness, love, empathy, generosity, and comprehension. It is on to you to start meeting those requirements if your spouse is unable to do so. Give yourself some grace and kindness. And remember that you are strong, and all you need to do is empower yourself in order to realize your goals and aspirations!

Live for yourself first and set yourself free. We're still working on your tale. Just a challenging phase remains. The moment has come to flip the page and find the motivation you need to go in the direction of transformation and change.

Don't look back or let regret or pain stop you from moving forward and achieving your goals.

Relationship Narcissists

Narcissists may be excellent leaders, musicians, sportsmen, celebrities, and extremely successful businesspeople, but when it comes to human relationships, they are complete failures. They have the ability to amass fortune, but they have no understanding how to cultivate relationships.

Any connection requires communication, empathy, concern, and the sharing of hopes and worries with the other person. However, since they are too preoccupied with themselves and their requirements, narcissists are unable to connect to or satisfy any of these parts of a relationship. No matter whether it's a narcissistic parent, lover, or sibling, they will never be able to really love anybody. They could seem to love people, but they don't really feel it.

Because they are unable to love themselves, narcissists find it impossible to love others. Even if they may be self-centered and selfish, they lack any meaningful relationships, even with themselves, which is why uncertainties, shame, and unidentified phobias have control over them. They merely want someone to prop up their egos; nothing else. If you say anything that they disagree with, they quickly get upset and furious. You almost feel like you have to tread carefully around them. You have two options: either compliment a narcissist or keep silent. They will feel threatened if you confront them or reveal your true thoughts. They don't see you as a unique person with your own ideas, viewpoints, and beliefs. They just see you as someone who must satisfy their demands.

Particularly damaging to close relationships is narcissism. It may be quite damaging to have a narcissistic parent or love partner. You turn becoming their go-to person for narcissistic supply. The connection has the potential to be deadly. While you may have the choice to leave a narcissistic spouse, you are still forced to spend a lot of time with them. Here is what to anticipate:

A narcissistic parent brags about their child's accomplishments in public but never offers them emotional support.

They frequently make excuses to avoid spending time with their children, get upset frequently, and put them under a lot of pressure. They act selfishly and ruthlessly, and never pardon their child if they find them doing something wrong.

Therefore, when someone grows up under such poor parental guidance, they either develop a severe lack of confidence and are unable to face life's challenges or they imitate their parents' actions and treat their future spouses and children in the same manner.

A narcissistic sibling feels that they are deserving of more esteem and adoration than their other siblings. They frequently exaggerate their own accomplishment to make the other person's success look smaller. Whenever the family comes together, they like to joke about how their physical beauty, abilities, intelligence, and achievements are superior than their younger or older siblings. Although they behave as if you are jealous of them, they are really envious of you.

A narcissist will often dismiss your emotions. Even when they seem to care, their primary concern is themselves. They don't take into account other people's preferences or will, basing all of their choices only on what will please them. They can also seek to isolate and control you. They can find it awkward that you have a separate group of pals and want to spend out with them. They can attempt to isolate you from your friends and even prevent you from pursuing your dream job. They won't necessarily tell you outright to live in accordance with them, but they will use deception to get what they want from you. You can eventually start to feel as if you've lost your individuality to appease a narcissist.

The hardest aspect of spotting a narcissist is that their pleasant demeanor makes you more inclined to be drawn to them at first. Finding love with a narcissist is not all that difficult. But as time goes on, people start to show their true selves in various circumstances. They aren't precisely who you first considered attractive, as you eventually find. Your mind will be blown, you'll be confused, and you'll start to question who you are. The terrible aspect is that you inevitably form an emotional and intellectually solid relationship with them. You find it perplexing because despite being a regular person, they want perfection from you and treat you poorly if you fall short.

Methods You Can Employ To End That Toxic Relationship

Leaving a bad relationship behind may not be easy or quick. But when you open up your life once again, everything will be alright.

There are numerous opinions on how to exit a toxic relationship, but they all boil down to this:

You proceed with caution.

The majority of the time, you'll need to spend a lot of time searching your soul, making arrangements, figuring things out, and then negotiating the perilous transition to another existence.

When you are motivated to quit that toxic relationship, it may be difficult to know where to start. It's important to find strategies to boost your own confidence and build an emotionally supportive network; if you feel stuck, it may be a good idea to speak with a therapist for further assistance.

Here, we walk you through specific actions to take in order to terminate a toxic relationship. For you, there can be more or fewer steps since every situation is different. You are unique. You have the chance to revert to that person right now.

1. Stop Living In Denial

Looking a problem in the eye is always the first step towards solving it. This is especially true when it comes to exiting harmful relationships.

It may seem a bit forward-thinking to acknowledge that you are in a poisonous relationship. It is, nevertheless, quite large.

From denial to acceptance, you are crossing a canyon.

You are capable of doing this.

2. Be aware of the benefits

It's possible that your unhealthy relationship may attempt to benefit you.

So, take out your journal and jot them down there. Which of these sounds familiar to you?

We split the cost. Living alone was too lonely for me.
She's very beautiful. In essence, she sometimes thinks.
Everything about my 60s is natural. How am I able to start my life over again?

Write out all of your justifications and benefits. Check to see whether the benefits are really worth the expense.

3. Fill in the gaps

After the benefits are gone, opportunities will arise in your life. It would be best to make plans now about how to top things off.

Let's suppose that owning a house is one benefit of your unhealthy relationship. You might start looking for other housing options, even if it means spending a short while sharing a bed with a friend or cousin.

If you have access to some extra cash, this may be the perfect time to start being flexible about taking on temporary or follow-up employment. Remind yourself that there are other fish in the water if friendship or perhaps love is an advantage.

Start in particular doing the things you've been putting off because of your relationship.

4. Acknowledge that you deserve better.

An person might get exhausted after receiving harsh treatment for months or a prolonged amount of time, and you can start to believe it. This isn't true in any scenario. The tactic used by abusive spouses to keep victims entangled in the relationship is to undermine confidence and self-esteem. Make "I merit better!" your daily mantra by replacing derogatory beliefs about your self-worth with affirming ones. For the sake of your own psychological well-being and immediate success, you should truly go forward.

5. Create A Point-by-Point Strategy

If you have made the decision to leave a toxic relationship, plan how you will handle the transition. If you don't already have a job, you should give attending classes, receiving new training, or beginning a job some serious thought. Financial independence is crucial to your opportunity. Define your plans for where you'll relocate, what property you'll take with you, and other details.

6. Create A Network Of Emotionally Supportive People

The feelings you go through after a toxic breakup are similar to those you go through in a healthy relationship. You'll experience misery, confusion, infatuation, ease, discouragement, and the list goes on from there. If you were financially dependent on your ex, ending a toxic relationship may be very difficult. However, don't give up.

Instead of focusing on the reasons why this would be difficult, concentrate on creating the network of emotional supporters you will need if you decide to leave. According to research, the support of family and friends through trying times reduces mental suffering. It will be easier for you to improve if you have an emotional support network to lean on.

7. Seek Skillful Support From a Therapist

Depending on how realistic the situation is, developing a plan for ending a toxic relationship may need assistance. It might also be beneficial to put your faith in loved ones or look for a therapist to chat to. A good therapist can help you with adjusting, rebuild your identity value, and handle any health concerns. A therapist may be a good tool to guide you and hold you accountable for setting goals and upholding them.

8. Let your emotions be known

When you decide to leave, it is crucial to let your spouse know how you feel. An in-person talk is best if your spouse is really evolved, but if they are irascible or near to home, working out your feelings may be preferable.

It's important to express how your relationship makes you feel without assigning blame. Avoid using things like "You make me feel..." and instead offer something like "I feel exceptionally miserable or furious when I hear you say... " to describe your sentiments.

Although you have no influence on how the other person responds, you do have some control over how you convey your emotions (in a neutral manner). Whatever their response, talking to them about how you feel is a crucial step towards ending the connection.

9. Maintain Your Position

After leaving a toxic relationship, it's common to miss the person, remembering only the good moments and forgetting the poisonous aspects. Although it could be tempting to want the person back in your life, keep in mind that you made the decision to leave after a careful consideration process and for important reasons.

Make contact with your social network of emotional support, as they will help you stay committed to your decision. Examine the factors that led you to end the unhealthy relationship, as well. Keep your resolve and stick to your decision.

10. End communication

You must cut off communication with your ex when the relationship has ended. Maintaining contact with your ex opens the door to reconciliation. Truly cunning manipulators, toxic people may use severe compulsion to keep you around them. Stop all contact with your spouse as soon as you decide to break up, with the exception of if you have children together and must co-parent. If so, simply mention the children.

Additionally, seeing your ex in online entertainment will keep the memories of the breakup fresh, so it's important to ban them on your phone and find other methods to avoid running into them in person. These exercises will help you establish a realistic cutoff point for the toxic connection and encourage you to stop thinking about it completely.

11. Let Go of Guilt

You could have regret after ending a toxic relationship for a variety of reasons. You could feel guilty because you:

Remaining too long in the relationship hurt the other party, the relationship had the potential to harm your children.

Whatever the reason you feel guilty, self-absolution is the first step toward healing.

You can sincerely and genuinely benefit from forgiveness.

Reconciliation can:

Reduce the risk of coronary failure.
Reduce Pulse
Develop cholesterol levels further
Reduce Stress, Anxiety, And Nervousness Levels

12. Say the affirmations again.

Affirmations are powerful tools for growth. Try telling yourself "I am strong" if you want to feel powerful in any particular areas, for instance. Obviously, you'll need to move in a useful manner as well!

When you practice normal self-affirmation, your brain really changes.

13. Surround Yourself With Positive Energy

Practice self-care by surrounding yourself with positive people. Spend time with people who inspire you. Indulge in your favorite meal. Attract people to your confidence-boosting environment. Exercise. Do activities that make you smile. People in toxic relationships need to be healed, which is a process that takes time. Being in a bad relationship may put a lot of stress on you, so it's important to try to replace depressing sentiments with positive ones.

14. Allow time for relaxation.

According to most relationship therapists, the best thing you can do after a breakup of any kind is to allow yourself some time to relax and recover. This is especially clear after a terrible relationship.

After you shut that section, take as much time as you need to breathe in and reaffirm your love for life.

Withdrawing from a habit-forming or poisonous relationship requires the same amount of willpower as going to work every day. In all honesty, this could be the most difficult task you have ever completed. Despite the support of those who understand your goal, you should lead a simple life for the rest of your days. You truly need some alone and relaxation.

A toxic relationship may be difficult and time-consuming to end. It may, however, also be empowering and freeing. It could provide you new opportunities in life.

Make sure you make the necessary, hefty expenditure to complete it. Even if you've been in the relationship for a time, it makes no difference. Typically, you have a strategy for leaving and a course of action you can take.

The supportive group of individuals you surround yourself with at work will help you finish.

Stay safe. Know your options if you anticipate even the slightest possibility of retaliatory abuse or viciousness.

Praise yourself for making it thus far before terminating off a poisonous relationship you're in. Remind yourself that you deserve a strong connection.

The Secret Narcissist

Many people mistakenly believe that narcissists are outgoing people. Although there is a lot of truth to this image, there are also introverted narcissists. Since they are more powerful, the extroverted narcissists are the focus of most of this book. However, in this chapter, you may get a glimpse into the thoughts of the hidden narcissist.

Psychologists claim that covert or "covert" narcissists take satisfaction in being seen as "sensitive" and "mysterious," but in truth, they are only trying to hide their fears and weakness by projecting this image. They exhibit the same severe neediness as their extroverted counterparts in this regard.

The Secret Narcissist's Characteristics

Secret narcissists are prone to becoming lost in their own thoughts and many anxieties. especially if they are quite shy under the spotlight, they are ready to claim credit for a success, especially if others assisted them. They believe their worries are too significant to be bothered by other people's issues. They like to be alone themselves and will only care to be with people if they openly welcome and appreciate them. Like the extroverted narcissist, covert narcissists are easily envious of others and become irritated if someone starts chatting with someone else in front of them.

The covert narcissist has a tendency to assess people too quickly and gives them grades based on how they treat him. Secret narcissists may be nasty and combative as well, particularly when they are challenged or experience failure. Secret narcissists avoid being rejected in any way. They often have a "me against the world" attitude and feel as if they are continually under pressure.

The capacity of the covert narcissist to put up a front in front of their true self makes them a little more effectively manipulating, which is one of the main ways in which they vary from the more extroverted one.

Introversion vs. The Secret Narcissist

How can the naturally shy individual be distinguished from the covert narcissist? Given that neither one expresses their true feelings, that is a challenging endeavor. The covert narcissist seems as reserved when, in reality, they are really very angry that no one else appreciates their genius. Finding out about each person's interests is one approach to distinguish between the two. An introverted person who sincerely enjoys helping animals or working for a cause, for instance, is most likely not a covert narcissist. On the other hand, the quiet person who writes only about herself in her private blog may in fact be a covert narcissist.

You think you done something wrong all the time.

One key characteristic of narcissism is the incapacity to take responsibility for any negative actions or harmful behavior.

The majority of the time, abusive spouses will find a way to blame you. They may deceive you in this way, typically by:

claiming that they said something that you don't recall them saying with great insistence.
getting so furious that you have to calm them down by saying you're sorry that you made a mistake.
Declare that you believe they cheated on you. You ask about the scenario and explain the unpleasant behaviors you have seen.

Narcissistic manipulation by a spouse may result in violent behavior. They could refute your accusations with their own, shift the blame, and say things to disparage and degrade you.

After these fits of rage, you could feel reliant and powerless and grateful that they are still wanting to be with someone who constantly makes errors.

Even after the relationship ends, you can still believe that you are incapable of doing any task well. You could start to blame yourself for problems that occur in other areas of your life.

Your bodily ailments have no known cause.

Abuse may make you nervous and worried, and sometimes that might manifest as physical symptoms.

You may notice:

an alteration in appetite.
stomach discomfort or nausea.

gastrointestinal symptoms, including soreness in the abdomen.
aches and pains in the muscles.
insomnia.
fatigue.

Sometimes it might seem like a good idea to use alcohol and other medicines, particularly sleeplessness, to address these symptoms. In an attempt to deal with negative feelings or physical pain, you can thus find yourself overindulging.

You feel restless and agitated.

Sometimes narcissistic abuse may be unexpected. Without your knowing, they could give you advice or a present.

You could feel extremely stressed out if you always need to be prepared for confrontation since you can never predict what someone else will do or say.

Additionally, you could always be on edge as you worry about how to respond to the unrelenting criticism and the abusive behaviors you're beginning to see. You may not know how to relax since you might not feel safe letting down your guard anymore.

Your self cannot be positioned.

When they are the target of abuse, many individuals progressively alter their self-identity to fit an abusive relationship.

When you go out with your friends, you're telling me you don't love me, your lover insists. You'd rather watch them, however.

Of course, you stopped hanging out with your friends because you love them. You finally quit coming to visit your sister each week and stop engaging in your hobbies. You also stop attending to happy hour with your colleagues after work. Since you take the time to fulfill their wishes, your spouse can know that you really care about them.

You may experience confusion and emptiness as a consequence of these alterations, which typically cause a loss of identity. It might be challenging to let go of your ambitions and have fun in life.

You find it difficult to draw limits.

Abusers who are narcissistic usually disregard boundaries. They could push your boundaries, ignore them totally, or remain quiet until you give up to their demands. Eventually, you could cease observing your limits at all.

You make a promise to yourself that you won't answer their calls or messages or otherwise communicate with them when you remove yourself from a narcissistic parent when you break up with them or do so.

They may not be as ready to let you go, however, if they think they might ultimately exhaust you. Instead, they'll keep calling and messaging you to try to talk you into going beyond of your boundaries once again.

If you have been the victim of narcissistic abuse, it may be challenging for you to establish appropriate boundaries in your dealings with others.

How To Deal With A Narcissist

There are eight strategies for handling narcissists. But first, since narcissists behave and respond differently, you need to be able to identify which kind you're dealing with.

Which Kind

A weak narcissist is not likely to have a very positive inner self-image. The emotions of a grandiose narcissist are less obvious, and you may not be aware that they are making you uncomfortable or getting in the way. The grandiose narcissist could be a terrific asset if you need someone to manage a team, but don't allow them make you seem bad.

Recognize Annoyance

Antagonizing behaviors from narcissists should no longer be ignored; instead, you should realize that they are grating on your nerves. Recognize that you are annoyed if the person you are working with constantly draws attention to themselves.

Recognize the source of their behavior From

A fragile narcissist is someone who needs to improve their own self-esteem, which is why they will start to be underhanded and cunning. They challenge authority and create trouble both at work and at home. When you see that they are uneasy, you may give them a little confidence so that they can concentrate and relax. Try not to over-reassure them since it will just fuel their ego fires.

Analyze the Context

Narcissism is a trait that may change as a person advances through their careers and throughout their life. Therefore, a narcissist may get agitated under certain circumstances. Therefore, until they have completed certain courses and improved their self-esteem levels, be conscious of what makes them feel uneasy and try to avoid such themes and behaviors.

Stay Upbeat

Showing someone who enjoys seeing others suffer the agony or anguish you could experience because of them won't help the situation; rather, it will make it worse. Smile through it and don't seem upset if they are irritating you or getting on your nerves. Subtly continue the discussion or completely exit the situation.

Do not veer off course

It's simple to become sidetracked by a narcissist's actions and forget your objectives or sense of purpose. Stop this from happening. Do not let anybody steal your focus or the spotlight away from you, no matter how hard they try.

Keep the humor up

When you utilize comedy to expose a narcissist's shortcomings, they will react favorably to it. When you are able to make a joke out of them hogging the attention or being a bit too over the top, it fosters a sense of shared understanding and trust with them. This is particularly useful when dealing with a partner, close friend, or family member.

Realize They Need Assistance

You have to understand that certain narcissists are going to require therapy since they have a propensity to have poor self-esteem. It's critical to realize when they want professional assistance since they really feel horribly inadequate. Narcissists may learn to be empathic and comprehend others around them, and they can alter long-standing tendencies. If you are not a professional, you should not attempt to boost their self-esteem on your own. Try to persuade them to get specialist assistance.

Keep in mind that narcissistic personality disorder is a serious and crippling condition. If you have this condition, there are people who can assist you. If you live with or are romantically associated with someone who has this illness, there is assistance available for both you and your partner.

The Origins & Mythology of Narcissism

Mythology

The work of Publius Ovidius Naso, often known as Ovid, a Roman poet who penned Metamorphoses, a large compilation of narrative mythology that covered 15 books, provides the finest "origin" tale that we may trace narcissism back to. The first appearance of the character Narcissus occurs in Book III of this collection. The most well-known beginning of what we now know as narcissism is Narcissus and the tale of him.

The narrative opens with Narcissus, a character from the southernmost section of the Peloponnesian Peninsula called Laconia, strolling through a mountain's forest. He is a hunter by profession and works in Thespiae. He is an attractive dude.

A mountain nymph observes Narcissus when he is strolling in the woods and falls in love with him. Being completely fascinated on the attractive and stunning guy she has caught her attention, she hides between the woods and stalks her new love. She adheres to him. Narcissus realized that he was being watched, whether because of his profession as a huntsman or because the lady rustled the leaves as she hopped from one tree to another or stepped on a stick that snapped and made noise. He stopped

and peered around. No one. But he sensed it. He shouted, "Who is there?"
Mountain echoes may be heard. It answered. It questioned, "Who is there?" The mountains were imitating him, echoing his words in a feminine manner. a female voice?
He asked again, "Who is there?" Nevertheless, the mountain's echo resembled a lady. He gave up, irritated and disappointed, and made the decision to disregard it and go on with his journey. The mountain nymph emerged from the shadows while he was doing this, her arms spread and her love as unconstrained as her dignity. She rushed up to Narcissus and touched his torso and arms. He was repulsed by this woman's disgusting lack of interest in males. He stopped her in her tracks. He yelled at the lady, telling her to get away. Hearing his words, the mountain nymph's heart splintered and broke. She

started crying as she saw Narcissus go. She collapsed to the ground, her tears becoming a distressed wail as she was overcome by emotion.

The mountain nymph would spend the rest of her days in shame and humiliation, haunted by the recollection of the attractive man who had turned down her love. She would pass away, leaving nothing but a scarcely heard echo as her last sound. This was her heartbreak—her soul's echo of the most agonizing moment she had ever experienced.

The tale of the mountain nymph known as Echo is told to Nemesis, the goddess of vengeance. Nemesis makes the decision that there is just one thing left to do since she can sense the woman's rage and anguish. Narcissus will be punished by Nemesis. Narcissus descends the mountain to get some water one day after a hard and strenuous day of hunting up there in the woods. Narcissus comes upon a body of water. He is unaware that Nemesis tricked him into going to this pool; he did not just stumble upon it. He lowers himself and holds out his hands to catch the first drips of water that could brush his lips. He then stops. He turns to face the sea, his eyes widening. His desire for refreshment diminished. Evaporated. Instead, such beauty was mirrored in the lake. A young man's reflection in the water caught Narcissus' attention because of his impressionable youth and good-looking austerity. Narcissus became fixated on the young man's reflection before realizing that it was indeed him. He was unable to exit the pool since he was his own reflection. He was enthralled and came to the realization that he was the only one capable of giving love from inside. Narcissus was so in love with himself at that very time that he had no desire to look away from himself. He remained; Nemesis's retribution was served. His human shape was replaced by a white and golden bloom in the exact location where he would ultimately dry and die, and all life inside him halted.

He was standing there beside the water, admiring his lovely and young reflection.

The Causes of Narcissism & What Characterizes a Narcissist

There are several ways to approach the roots that take hold of someone and mold them into individuals who exhibit extreme narcissism. There are underlying problems and traumas that they experienced or grew up with. Mental, physical, and sexual abuse are all possible forms of abuse someone may have experienced. They may have had a parent who was irresponsible as a child, forcing them to "grow up" quickly and by themselves. They might have been the victims of a horrific crime or tragic accident, or they might have grown up with a narcissist (a parent, sibling, or other adult), in which case they may have become a sponge for the personality and behavior of those people. The unpleasant and sometimes sad exposure to adult issues that leave lasting mental scars provides the grounds for narcissistic behavior to develop in a person. Another possibility is that they were constantly lavished with unmerited praise, which gave them the impression that they could never fail, which is considered to be the main defect of narcissists.

Lack of empathy from a parental figure is one of the factors that might cause narcissism to manifest in children. According to studies, kids who don't get enough love don't grow up with the skills necessary to know how to love others back. Given that the youngster is not getting enough attention at home, this behavior may first manifest as a demand for more attention. The act of acting out or flaunting oneself in order to attract attention might then intensify. Additionally, a young youngster could start to think that being kind inevitably results in a reward. This detracts from the act of kindness and could lead to a mistaken expectation that compassion will always be appreciated.

Why Do Children Become Selfish?

It's a frequent belief that narcissistic children are horrible kids, however this is untrue. Human nature dictates that kids are innately selfish. A young person's fundamental expectation is to have their needs addressed. When this is distorted, it may be a very perplexing stage in a child's development. Narcissism might start to take shape in this way. It is a battle for growth as much as a scream for attention. In contrast to women, males have NPD at a higher rate. A growing kid already feels the pressure of expectations from society that are set at a young age. Boys are often seen to be more resilient and less emotional. The unmet demands often appear as dangerous behaviors as a result of this buried perplexity.

The activities are changed to a clamoring need for attention in lieu of being able to voice demands and wishes. If narcissism persists throughout adulthood, it may become very difficult to cure. A youngster often outgrows their inherent selfishness and develops understanding and appreciation. The selfish phase never ends in narcissism, which functions differently. Instead, a feeling of entitlement is present. It is not unexpected that a youngster will do everything to obtain additional attention and recognition if they don't feel worthy. Early detection of this conduct is crucial to avoiding it from becoming NPD. A psychologically sound youngster should learn that choices have consequences as they become older. A youngster should be aware that their value is never in doubt, not even while they are receiving punishment. Although it is felt, empathy is also taught. Children must be taught by their parents that their actions have consequences for other people. This is an essential stage in helping children develop a broad variety of emotional depth.

Bullying: Children that bully others usually have some kind of internal problem. Making fun of or picking on other kids might be a method for someone with a superiority complex to show off. Children who are bullied may get the power-hungry gratification they want.

White falsehoods are one thing, but telling lies repeatedly for one's own benefit may turn into a very destructive habit. It becomes a severe problem when a youngster learns how to continue telling falsehoods in exchange for anything else.

Lack of Accountability: Narcissistic children often struggle to accept that they are in error. It is simple to point the finger at others while never accepting responsibility for one's own conduct. A youngster may not be able to understand the difference between right and wrong if they experience this sort of frequent deflection.

Aggression: This attitude may show itself in any circumstance, not only bullying. A youngster acting aggressively out of the ordinary is often a sign that something is setting off the reaction.

Because a narcissistic youngster will struggle to articulate their feelings, the reply is often cruel or disregarded.

Undying A narcissistic kid will do whatever it takes to win. Both academic settings and informal fun with friends may benefit from this. Even if others suffer as a result, the need for attention often takes precedence over empathy.

Egotistical attitudes: When a youngster exhibits egotism, narcissistic behaviors will undoubtedly follow. Be on the lookout for a strengthened sense of self that is prioritized above other emotions.

Intolerance of collaboration: Children might sometimes be difficult, but a persistent intolerance of collaboration is a bad indicator. A crucial aspect of infancy is learning who the authoritative figure is—the parent. The cycle of narcissism will never cease if a youngster learns that parents are not required to be followed.

Possessing Special Expectations: Children who believe they should get preferential treatment over others are more prone to have conflicting ideas about their value. Those who anticipate this treatment, even when it is unjustified, exhibit narcissistic traits. Yes, excellent conduct should be commended, but not at the expense of other people's needs; this is a lesson that has to be imparted.

Trauma And Narcissistic Bonding

The phrase simply denotes a relationship formed between two individuals as a result of hardship. Positive outcomes include friends becoming closer as a consequence of sharing a tragic event like the loss of a loved one. However, with a narcissist, the bonding happens as a result of the ongoing cycle of abuse and reconciliation, which solidifies the connection while also emotionally tying the victim of abuse to their abuser and changing how they see intimacy.

Intermittent reinforcement is the word used to describe this. The abuser will sometimes intersperse periods of intense love with their typical abusive conduct in an abusive relationship. An abusive narcissist would, for instance, purchase jewelry for his humiliated girlfriend during a family function. It makes the sufferer dependent on searching for such tokens of affection and wishing for a revival of the marriage's bygone honeymoon phase.

Trauma bonding takes the form of the victim opening up to and being vulnerable for the narcissist in a manner that they would recognize as poisonous if they saw a friend doing it.

However, for the victim, it seems like a whole new level of closeness, and it feels fantastic, at least initially, to the point where other relationships seem insignificant in contrast. However, this supposedly higher degree of closeness eventually turns out to be a lie. It is in no way intimate. Co-dependence is a risky situation for persons who are close to an abusive narcissist.

Trauma Bonding Signs

If you are stuck in an abusive relationship with a narcissist and find it

difficult to leave them, trauma bonding may be to blame. Do you fit any of the following descriptions?
- Compatibility issues with others.
- Feeling exhausted.
- Uncertainty.
- Conflict about unimportant issues.
- Concern that you may have given the narcissist too much.
- Thinking that your loved ones don't comprehend your connection.
- Sensing that you'll never be able to appease the narcissist.
- Prioritizing the narcissist in your life above other crucial aspects.
- Believing that no one else can relate to you in such a profound way.
- Attempting to end the connection causes such excruciating suffering that you fear death.

Even if they never do anything, you can count on the narcissist to uphold their promises.

There is hope that you can leave a violent relationship if you see these indications in your life, but it will need hard effort and dedication.

Case Study: Janet and Brad

Brad believed he had found the ideal partner in Janet. He believed he would spend the rest of his life with her as their relationship immediately took off. They have two kids and almost ten years of marriage. Everything was wonderful during the honeymoon phase, but then everything began to change. Brad would often remark, "I always wondered why I was the only one she treated poorly."

Except for Ellen, Brad's mother, who didn't earn enough money to live on her own, it seemed that Janet had more regard for other people. This led to a significant lot of conflict since Janet believed Ellen was always staring at her and had unpleasant tendencies. It became worse to the point that Ellen had to move into her own apartment. When the cost prevented that, the debate that followed resulted in Janet hitting Ellen. Janet naturally assigned all of the responsibility to Brad.

Brad resorted to booze when things were so awful and even pondered committing himself. As soon as the grief from his divorce subsided, he started misusing painkillers. He lost his work as a result of his anxiety and depression when he requested a leave of absence to enter therapy. According to Brad, "they all lied to me, pretended to be my friends to get the information, only to use it against me in order to help them fire me." Brad learned that Janet had been having other affairs at this time as well.

After some time, Janet grabbed the kids and left, lamenting Brad's drug use and declaring it to be intolerable. Brad, who is now left to pick up the pieces, worries that his children may be developing the same issues he experienced.

Again, Janet blamed Brad for everything, even though it was the result of her narcissistic abuse, including the business with his mother, the adultery, the mental health problems, and the drug and alcohol misuse.

A Closer Exam

Brad had a number of characteristics linked to narcissistic abuse syndrome. He was unable to escape the predicament. One would assume that he would have reached the point of giving up when Janet smacked his mother on top of everything else going wrong. No, he didn't. He most likely explained this by claiming that his children needed him, but it's also possible that he would have remained even if there were no children there.

He had little faith in anybody and assumed the worst in all around him, particularly his employees. Although this could indicate that Brad exhibits some narcissism, it's important to keep in mind that his home life had left him depleted. Brad resorted to drugs and alcohol to try to relieve the agony as his life was falling apart and he was struggling to cope, but this just made things worse.

To put it another way, this formerly content and successful person lost himself and reduced to nothing more than a warped mirror of the perception of him that his narcissistically abusive wife held.

Brad and anybody else experiencing abuse from a narcissist must keep in mind that it is not their fault. It is not your fault if you are reading this and identifying your suffering in these tales. Being a victim of violence is not shameful, just as having narcissistic abuse syndrome is not shameful.

Someone you trusted wounded you, and they ought to have been the last person in the world to do you any damage. As a result, you are the victim. Narcissistic abuse syndrome may be excruciating and confusing, but it can also be prevented and addressed.

Have you been the victim of narcissistic abuse?

There are several signs you may look for that, if present, signal that you should think about seeking treatment, even though a real diagnosis can only be obtained from a qualified therapist. The narcissistic abuse syndrome symptoms provide the basis for the questions that follow. The likelihood that you have it increases with the number of "Yes" responses you have.

Do your experiences seem dissociated from you? The traditional symptoms of trauma include feeling emotionally or physically cut off from your surroundings, as well as having issues with perception, memory, or your sense of self. In order to filter out the pain and conceal the true horror of your circumstance, related thoughts and sensations are compartmentalized. This might result in undesirable behaviors including addiction, obsessions, suppression, and other means of numbing the pain.

Do you constantly exercise caution while you are in the presence of your abuser? In an effort to prevent repeating the trauma, it is usual to avoid everything that is related to it. This entails being very conscious of your words and actions around your abuser and adapting them to avoid offending them. It is a pointless exercise since the abuser's emotional ebbs and flows, not you, what you say, or what you do, are what create the abuse. Your capacity to be assertive, establish boundaries, and cultivate good relationships is undermined by this conduct.

Do you give up your identity for your abuser? In abusive relationships, particularly those involving a malignant narcissist, it is typical for the abuser to totally engulf every area of the victim's life, causing them to overlook their own fundamental wants and desires in order to obtain the abuser's approval and admiration. Your hopes and aspirations vanish, and your relationships with friends and family deteriorate—all to the narcissist's detriment. Why? Because a narcissist cannot find satisfaction.

How To Spot A Narcissistic Mother Right Away

It's a huge thing to label someone a narcissist, yet most narcissists aren't shy about letting their presence be known. In this chapter, we'll discuss the many signs of narcissistic personality disorder and the narcissistic characteristics that characterize it in general. We'll also develop an awareness of how these characteristics may, regrettably, define your connection with your parent(s).

Do keep in mind that not all toxic relationships are narcissistic, despite the fact that the majority of them are. While your parents may or might not engage in the activities described in this chapter, there's a strong likelihood that you already have a poisonous and/or tense connection with them if you felt the need to read this book in the first place. As a result, remember that even if your connection with your parents doesn't exhibit all the characteristics of a narcissistically poisonous nature, you will probably still gain from the suggestions in this book that deal with coping, healing, and cutting in terms of the relationship.

The following symptoms are often shown by someone with narcissistic personality disorder, however many times all or most of them are present. We'll go through each of these signs individually so you can comprehend what they are and how they could especially affect a loved one.

The emergence of great grandiosity is the first sign. In a psychological setting, grandiosity is defined as having an exaggerated sense of oneself and exaggerated ideas of what one has personally done or is capable of. This necessitates the fact that someone with a grandiose personality would likewise demand to be treated differently from other individuals.

It's a bit difficult to predict how this would show out in parental relationships. In general, you could think of your parent as being conceited if they are always talking about how great they are and preoccupied with themselves. They may grumble if you don't prioritize them over other people or things in your life, when you don't heed their advise, or when you don't take the precise course they want you to take because they want you to treat them differently.

The second sign is that they will be preoccupied with ideals of being extraordinarily strong, gorgeous, successful, intelligent, etc. This may show up in a variety of ways. The tendency for narcissistic personality disorder and narcissism in general to foster great ambition may be a double-edged sword since it can strain family relationships if a parent withdraws and neglects you in favor of their career. Furthermore, because of their fascination with power, they can attempt to exert a lot of control over you and your life. If you don't give them complete power over you and all you do, they could get too enraged and seek to dominate you at all costs. Because this is generally a dead giveaway, be cautious of its possible effect.

They may attempt to influence you at times by making it seem as if their desire to have total control over you is in your best interests. You should attempt to recall instances in the past when this has occurred and be actively alert that it may happen. You most definitely have a narcissist on your hands if it seems that the things they wish to perform are only motivated by their own wants or perceptions of themselves in relation to you.

The third sign is that they believe themselves to be particularly exceptional, superior, or associated with others who are strong or at the top of the social scale. They may be acting narcissistically if they make an effort to boast about how popular or outstanding they are or if it is obvious from their conduct that they believe they are the greatest but are unable to provide the credentials to support such claims. Until they use it to degrade you, make you feel inferior, or give you a reason to be obedient, this is one of the least troublesome things. Recognize this and any implications it could have for your interaction with your narcissistic parent. The fourth indication is their persistent demand for affirmation and admiration from others. This may show up in a variety of ways. They could continually act in a way to get your approval or they might portray themselves as superior than they really are so that you grow to appreciate them. They may respond harshly or even in a destructive, abusive manner by lashing out at you either physically or emotionally if you don't give them the respect they need.

The fifth sign is related to the first in that a narcissistic personality disorder sufferer will have a strong feeling of entitlement. They will intentionally get angry or offended if they don't get the special treatment they believe they are continually entitled to. They'll also demand compliance from others all the time. A narcissist will hold it over your head if you defy them and either punish you severely right away or attempt to make you feel very terrible. Additionally, it's not unusual for them to gaslight you later on into believing that events transpired differently or to hold your disobedience over your head to shame you into acting in the future.

The sixth sign is their willingness to take advantage of others if it means they will profit from it. The fact that they just care about themselves and their own approval is what makes dealing with this one of the most irritating things to do. Although this characteristic appears oddly Machiavellian, it makes perfect sense in the disorder's larger framework. This, along with the complete absence of empathy outlined later, may often distinguish someone who is just narcissistic from someone who is genuinely suffering from narcissistic personality disorder. However, this often has a significant impact on their personal relationships. If it means getting their way, they will manipulate you shamelessly, and they aren't hesitant to use you as a tool.

The seventh symptom is related to the last one: those who have narcissistic personality disorder often either reject empathy for others or have limited empathy. It's interesting to note that in comparison to individuals who do not have clinical narcissism, brain studies on people with narcissistic personality disorder have revealed that the area of their brains associated with empathy and connection to others is frequently stunted or generally shrinks. As a result of their seeming deliberate disregard for your emotions, this may be one of the most unpleasant aspects of living with a narcissistic parent. They very well may not, is the straightforward response. The most extreme narcissists utilize you just to support their exaggerated ideas of themselves; they don't really use you for anything else. They could even consider you a drain.

The narcissist's worldview is the subject of the ninth symptom. Generally speaking, the narcissist will be intensely envious of the possessions or characteristics of others. This is so that the narcissist may have the finest of everything, be the greatest at everything, and enjoy the fame and adulation that comes with it. This may also apply in reverse. Since they believe they are the finest, they often believe that others want to be like them and desire what they possess. This specific feature may cause a lot of disruption. They could attempt to stifle your personal connections out of envy and a desire for power. They might even acquire an exaggerated fear of losing your affections, which paradoxically might fuel your hatred.

Simple: A narcissist often exhibits extreme arrogance. They often take steps to silence anyone who have beliefs that vary from their own and only accept their own particular view of how things should be done. They'll often strive to elevate themselves and their thoughts above others in talks and in everyday life, and they'll frequently be haughty and arrogant. This may be a reflection of your overzealous efforts to manage your life, such as when you are forbidden from dating someone for no legitimate reason other than arbitrarily superficial considerations like their social background.

With that, we have identified the key signs of narcissism. These things may have a significant influence on the growth of the children in the home, and it's not unusual for them to start to veer toward abuse.

This is due to the fact that narcissists, and particularly those who suffer from narcissistic personality disorder, only care about the individuals they are manipulating or abusing as a means to an end—the inflated growth of their own ego. In narcissistic situations, physical violence is unusual but not unheard of; instead, they favor generalized emotional and mental assault. First off, these abuses are far more subtle and are less likely to be seen as hazardous or undesired by the victim or by others who are around the narcissist in general. Additionally, it works better for the narcissist's overarching objectives. The narcissist seeks approval, as well as what ultimately amounts to the most devotion and power. The narcissist's mental abuse techniques—guilt, gaslighting, and manipulation—serve as a far superior route to achieve these objectives.

The reality that your parent's narcissism is to blame for these things may be very tough to see and accept. It might be difficult to acknowledge to yourself that you have experienced some kind of emotional abuse. These, however, are critical phases of the healing process.

The Severe Narcissistic Sadistic Mothers

These mothers lock up their kids in their rooms. They are often alcoholics and completely neglectful. They let the streets raise their children and don't care what happens to them. There is a tremendously deep level of abandonment.

Sometimes there are a series of new husbands. These step- fathers sometimes sexually abuse these kids, creating an unhealthy environment to raise a child. So many families don't deserve to raise kids because they simply will not provide a safe environment.

Unfortunately, the result of that is a very high number of people raised this way learn to fend for themselves. They have been shattered inside because they haven't received the sustenance, love, compassion, and protection they needed as children by virtue of being born.

Adult children of this kind of narcissistic mother will surely have a Complex Post Traumatic Stress Disorder (CPTSD).

The Enmeshed Mother

She is the most covert narcissistic mother. Instead of teaching you to build a life of your own, she snaps on the emotional handcuffs and never lets you go.

Emotional mothers can seem like they're just perfect, always taking care of their kids, but instead are turning their children into life long infants.

The enmeshed mother will never allow you to grow up. If you're a man you'll always be stuck between this half man-half child situation. Children in this situation are emotionally stunted in so many ways because they have been imprinted with the message that it's not safe outside of the home, and that it is always better to be here with mom.

This is a form of co-dependency training that doesn't allow the children to go out there and learn the skills of survival and assertiveness in order to succeed. Their independence is not being supported and instead they are being punished for trying to be self-sufficient.

This can be extremely damaging for men, especially boys, because there's a borderline component here and that is the fear of abandonment. The narcissistic mother wants to pour all of her love, all of her attention into the kids and make them the centre of her world and oftentimes this is a result of a bad relationship with the father of her children.

If the father isn't gone, most of the time he neglects the children. He neglects his wife especially, and she will turn him into a monster in the boy's eyes, and the boy is then going to take over the burden of the dad who is not present.

So the son is going to have to grow up very quickly and will be rewarded for being there for his mommy. He will essentially become her surrogate husband. It's something that's called parentification.

This sometimes creates really sensitive, openhearted and giving men, but the problem is that their boundaries are very permeable. There is not enough give-and-take in the relationship and they will just work themselves to the bone to satisfy a woman, because that's what they did for their mothers. They will take that outside of the relationship with their mom and continue this dynamic in their romantic relationships.

The problem with this is that it's very easy for other narcissists, sociopaths, psychopaths, and borderline women to be attracted to this kind of man and then destroy him.

These adult children of enmeshed narcissistic mothers will feel really hurt deep inside because they are like, "I'm doing everything I can, I'm the better version of myself, my mom raised me with the right values and yet I keep getting my ass kicked. Why?" Now you know why.

So, the enmeshing mother may think in her mind that she's doing the right thing but she's not; she is suffocating her children. A healthy relationship between a parent and a child, especially a mother and a child, has to come from respect and the giving of space.

Children need to feel like they can fully be themselves and develop to whatever seed they were, so they can become the person that they were meant to become. A good healthy parent will support that independence and that separation.

Techniques Of Command And Control

Gaslighting

The other partner's reality is continuously questioned and changed in a relationship with a narcissist. Conversations will be utterly misremembered when recounted in the future. If a victim ever told a narcissist, "You are hurting me," the narcissist may easily distort it into a darker version of the original dialogue, saying, "I enjoy hurting you." Gaslighting is a destructive process that involves several factors. One of them is the narcissist's blatant boldness, which the victim notices. Shock quickly gives way to despair, however, since the narcissist is unyielding in her pursuit of undermining the self-assurance and sanity of her spouse, friend, relative, or kid.

The Silent Approach

The narcissist will use "stonewalling" and the silent treatment to restrict the information that is shared with her victim. Keep in mind that the narcissist is never concerned with the thoughts or emotions of her victim. The victim is not a genuine person to the narcissist; rather, they are only a source of stimulation, which the narcissist might sometimes choose to turn off by interrupting a discussion at the outset.

Blaming

In an effort to make you feel bad, he will assign you the responsibility. He will provide the impression that you are to blame for everything and that you caused it all. You refused to engage in sexual activity, you were such a whiner, you placed your profession ahead of him, you took on weight, you whined excessively, and so on. He'll persuade you that you caused him to become evil and that's why he did it. He can persuade you that he is speaking the truth and persuade you to give him your supply once again.

The theatrical psychological games that narcissists typically start are often played at your cost. They have the ability to incite conflict between you and others, and once you are at each other's throats, they will act as if they had nothing to do with it. You should back off if you think a narcissist is using some form of psychological trick to provoke an angry response from you.

Narcissists relish the turmoil that results from their schemes, which is why they play games and instigate drama. When a narcissist initiates a fight between two people, he or she feels superior to them and acts as if they are puppets being controlled by the narcissist, who is acting as if they are god over your life. Let's look at some of the typical games that a narcissist may attempt to get you engaged in before you fall into the trap that the narcissist lays for you and end yourself entangled in a drama whose beginning you can't even recall.

Narcissists often engage in the "emotional ping pong" game. When someone deflects accountability for their acts back to you, they are avoiding accepting responsibility for their own actions. In the event that the narcissist does a repugnant behavior, he or she will somehow return the favor to you rather than taking responsibility for their acts and apologizing. He or she may attempt to place the responsibility on you, embarrass you, assign guilt to you, or even flatly deny doing anything improperly, making you seem insane for even bringing it up. You can find yourself believing the lie and even making excuses on their behalf if you care about him or her.

Projecting

The fact that survivors of relationships with narcissists question if they were or still are the narcissist is one of the most amazing, long-lasting consequences that they display.

How does one get from seeing and experiencing the terrible suffering a narcissist does to thinking that they, too, are capable of such brutality? "Projecting" is the term for the response to that query.

The would-be victim often pours the contents of their emotions to the narcissist during the courting or love-bomb period of a relationship with them, talking about prior heartache, being betrayed, being lied to, and having things taken from them. If the narcissist is told about any unpleasant events in the victim's background, he will reserve that information for a later time in the relationship when it will reappear as projection.

Twisting

One of the so-called "twisting" techniques they use most often is this one. The issue here is that, although words often mean one thing in dictionaries, they frequently signify something quite different to narcissists. Like a fish in the turbulent currents, the narcissist's language veers and turns. When you confront them about being overbearing, they will quickly refute your accusation and claim that they are "trying to look out for you" and "want what's best for you."

'Love bombing'

The typical initial step in dating is this. To get you to let down your guard and think he really does love you, he will drop "bombs" of notes, texts, calls, gifts, flowers, and chocolates throughout the day. Even if you may perceive some sincerity in his love bombing, you choose to ignore it and go with the flow.

You start to grow enamored with the attention and turn into a simple mark for his final attempt to manipulate and dominate you.

Objectification

This is one of the cruelest ways a narcissist can degrade their victim, and they do it out of pure inability to perceive people as whole human beings. Because they only genuinely have total control over items, narcissists reduce those who are close to them to becoming simply objects.

An item, such as a watch, vehicle, home, or piece of art, might be loved by a narcissist, but you can't love a person the same way you love a "thing" since loving someone takes empathy and understanding.

Psychological Blackmail

The narcissist often resorts to "emotional blackmail" to force their lovers or other people they care about to comply with their wishes and demands. In other words, the narcissist will threaten the victim with things that will make the victim feel fearful, guilty, or regretful.

When threatening their spouse, a narcissist may say something like, "If you ignore me like this, I'm going to kill myself." Or, if they are in drug rehab, the narcissist may make threats to get more drugs or shoot up once again to dull the sting of your betrayal.

Neglect The narcissist might treat their victim with neglect, which is the antithesis of emotional blackmail. Numerous factors often lead to neglect. The narcissist finds it challenging and often draining to communicate with others who are not suffering from mental disorders. So that they have one person with whom they don't have to be normal around, they often target one victim at a time. They own and are in charge of their victim, and they have a vast collection of knowledge and weapons at their disposal in case any issues occur. These resources are unavailable to the narcissist in comparison to the rest of humanity.

Mirroring

He will continually highlight your similarities in an effort to persuade you that you are quite similar to one another. Trapping you is crucial to the narcissist. He will concur with everything you say, laugh at all your jokes, and declare he enjoys the same foods, literature, and entertainment as you do in an effort to win you over.

Getting Into Your Privacy

Because they have nothing to hide if they leave their doors wide and unlocked, narcissists will urge that their victims do the same. They will search through the mail, emails, internet history, and dresser drawers of their victims. They could often go through their victim's phone to make assumptions about messages and phone conversations, then use those assumptions as justification for disputes and physical altercations.

Online searches for a victim's identity by a narcissist looking for information about their background may also be used as material for interrogation and insults.

Damage to Your Reputation

Character assassination is a skill that narcissists excel at. To feel better about their shortcomings, they will drop blatant bombs on social media and befriend your friends to create unfavorable stories about you. If you possess what the narcissist desires, such as a better career, home, vehicle, or spouse, the narcissist may get agitated and attempt to humiliate you. You must always be one level below the narcissist if you are their spouse in all facets of life.

When two people are in a narcissistic relationship, only one of them may be superior.

Triangulation

He sets you and another person up in a triangle—a parent, a colleague, a mistress, or a child—and positions you two against one another. This absolves him of responsibility while effectively making you anxious to maintain your connection. He wipes his hands clean as he observes the argument between the two of you.

Codependency Strengthening

Throughout a relationship with a narcissist, cycles of consoling and assaulting occur. As she assaults you more often, the more she comforts you, until she becomes both the cause of your suffering and your source of comfort, leaving you without any other important people in your life. Once your sense of reason and independence have been fully undermined to the point of blindness and absolute reliance on the narcissistic abuser, you could even stop wanting anybody else.

Disorder Of Narcissistic Behavior

This is perhaps the most damaging personality disease for a marriage or relationship, along with borderline personality disorder, for reasons that will soon become evident. Additionally, while borderline personality disorder is more prevalent in women, narcissists are often males. Not necessarily entirely, but more often.

The narcissist presents as the one who is infallibly correct. They always know the solutions to any problem. They appear to simply want to connect to themselves because they are so fully and entirely focused on themselves. They are so engrossed in their own world that they are unable to connect to their spouse very well and are also lacking in empathy. A narcissist is someone who tends to be very self-absorbed and preoccupied with themselves. They tend to their own requirements. They are not at all adept at playing the role of the other person or placing themselves in their partner's position. They lack compassion for the suffering of others.

Grandiosity is another trait of narcissists, especially when it comes to their intelligence and future plans. Though a narcissist always has the upper hand, it's crucial to keep in mind that not all righteous people are narcissists. Here, caution is advised, since narcissism is not a simple term to define accurately.

Being in a relationship with a narcissist is very challenging since they are always right. They will always assume the higher moral ground and explain to their partners why their partners—and not themselves, of course—need to get their act together. In other words, they approach the relationship with a deity-like perspective and, like the borderline, they don't see much, if anything, about how they contribute to the issues. In most cases, they will say to their spouse, "You're the issue. You must organize yourself. Of course, narcissists don't just say that; they also refuse to accept much responsibility for the chaos they bring about in the relationship.

As you may already be aware, there is often a significant overlap between borderline and narcissistic personality disorders. In reality, it's not unusual for someone to exhibit both traits, or at least some of them. Of course, this nearly tenfold increases the difficulties of working with such a person. It may make maintaining a relationship very difficult.

Between the two illnesses, there are, however, significant distinctions as well. Although narcissists have a tendency to be emotional, they are not often self-righteous or entirely self-focused. Because they don't usually respond emotionally to everything, they tend to be more clinical (which is one of the reasons why most narcissists are male because the logical rather than emotional response tends to be more of a masculine feature).

Narcissists defend their "rightness" logically rather than emotionally. In fact, they often consider that being too emotional is an insufficient way to live and frequently look down upon others who exhibit it. As a result, they may be quite critical of an emotional person. When someone expresses emotion, a narcissist may get irate, demanding, and judgmental of them. A borderline personality, on the other hand, tends to become more defensive than self-righteous. In actuality, they will employ emotion as their first and primary line of both offense and defense.

I warn against assuming someone has this personality condition right away once again. For instance, a person with a narcissistic inclination is nonetheless capable of connecting with others and repairing relationships. While I attempt to summarize the general traits of some of the most destructive personality disorders in this book (such as narcissism), it is advisable to seek a professional opinion or conduct thorough research before assuming that a given label will apply to your spouse.

Solutions For Narcissistic Personality Disorder

It's unclear how or why someone develops a narcissistic personality disorder, much as with borderline personality disorder. There is just insufficient data available. There is some evidence to show that emotional abuse as a kid (often by a parent who may also be a narcissist) might contribute to the condition. I have, however, also seen situations in which identically raised siblings from the same parents only had one of them become narcissistic.

identifying what to do about it, however, is more crucial than identifying the reason. How do you handle a scenario when your spouse, whether or not they are extreme, employs self-righteousness and rational support of their own stance and doesn't seem to budge or even see your side of the story?

Once again, the first step is to express to your spouse your worries about their "patterns of behavior." Wait until they are more composed, then gently bring up the matter without being critical or aggressive. Talk about how it makes you feel when they don't listen to you or don't seem to be thinking about your emotions.

Sadly, there is a drawback to this strategy. A narcissist often responds to questions about their conduct with a highly hostile response. The narcissist may be pretty aloof and not want to talk about it at all since they are not very emotionally engaged and don't care or feel pity for the other person.

Therefore, it is quite challenging for a narcissist's spouse to believe that the other person would pay attention to their feelings. The issue is that, in the end, a relationship can only be gratifying and rewarding when you have a partner who can pay attention to your sentiments, take them seriously, and support and assist you in them. It will be difficult for someone who lacks empathy to achieve that. And a person who is with a narcissist will often be aware of it. They will be aware that there is no escape route. They will experience extreme frustration trying to elicit an emotional response from their narcissistic spouse, and they will get so upset by the rejection that they will shut down. If communication ever actually happened in the first place, it stops at this point. When married to a narcissist, there may be a façade of "I'm happy" but that is merely a coping mechanism. There will be grief, regret, and maybe even anger, within. It's a very challenging circumstance for someone to be in.

What Is the Outlook for Your Marriage With Borderline and Narcissistic Behavior?

For the simple fact that they are the most prevalent and damaging of the severe personality disorders, I have concentrated on borderline and narcissistic personality disorders in this book. They both have significant effects on a marriage. And it will be obvious to you that none of them have a remedy. In all but the mildest situations, the 'sufferer' is unable to recognize their issue, hence they will never see the need to take action to alter their behavior. No matter what you do, they will always believe that there is nothing wrong with them since it is ingrained in their thinking and worldview. You just won't be able to persuade them differently, and attempting to do so would make you insane and lower your self-esteem.

So what is the outlook for such a union or partnership? Are partnerships that have these elements more likely to endure? Can you coexist peacefully with someone who suffers from one or more of these personality disorders?

In general, most spouses in a marriage may improve their communication skills. Most individuals are willing to pick up new skills, listen more intently, and grasp their partner's style of operating when issues emerge.

However, if a person is married to someone who is unwilling to work on themselves or their relationship with the goal of transforming and strengthening their marriage, they face challenges. Realistically, relationships are a two-way street. Both parties must acknowledge the need of making improvements. Good connections are made. On developing good partnerships is done. A couple who really wants to work through their disagreements and figure out how they can do things better will end up with a good relationship. Unfortunately, not everyone is capable of doing that. And those who suffer from narcissistic or borderline personality disorders are simply unable to accomplish it.

If you find yourself in a circumstance where you realize your spouse suffers from these personality disorders, you must accept the truth that maintaining the relationship will cost you dearly. A wonderful relationship won't 'become' one with you. You must acknowledge that you will never be completely happy while dating a borderline or a narcissist if you desire a marriage or relationship that makes that feasible. At best, you'll survive; at worst, your mental state will be completely devastated.

If you divorce or break up with one of these folks, you will pay a steep price.

These folks will do whatever it takes to 'prove' to you and to everyone else that you were very, very wrong to wish to leave your marriage,' therefore it is not unusual for someone to lose all they have. After all, they are in perfect health! Unfortunately, the fact that you want to go is an indication that there could be a problem with them, and they just cannot stand to think that there might be. Therefore, even while it comes at a cost to them as well, their retaliation against you will likely be planned, vicious, and intended to cause you as much suffering as possible.

However, consider the following: "If I had to pick just one thing to keep, which would it be—my soul or everything I own?"

You will lose your soul if you remain with a borderline or narcissistic person. Because these are the things your spouse will gradually whittle away at, you will lose your sense of self and your respect for yourself.

What is the point of sticking if you can frankly admit to yourself that you cannot see how your marriage might make you happy? Many individuals seem willing to do that, but staying or leaving comes with a cost.

Are you willing to put yourself first in order to be the greatest version of yourself, to pursue happiness, and to live your life to the fullest? Are you prepared to admit that the reason you are here is because you deserve to be supported in being who you actually are?

Because it's not common knowledge that individuals might be married to someone who has a personality problem, writing this book has been incredibly challenging. After all, they fell in love with that person at some time, and they probably still do. When you consider the fact that you can never be completely happy with someone who has these issues, it seems incredibly challenging.

However, I strongly advise you to respect yourself first while deciding what to do. What would you advise if one of your children approached you for guidance when you were in their shoes? If the relationship was doomed, would you advise them to remain and try to repair it, or would you advise them that what mattered most was their happiness?

There is a bright side to everything, however.

Because holding on to what you have feels safe and a little bit dangerous, people often desire to keep what they have. But everyone of us has to reflect on whether the quality of our lives with this person is what we want it to be. Will it truly be something that I can look back on and feel that I've had a happy life if I spend the rest of my life in the relationship I'm in?

You will be astonished by how much better your life will become if you can muster the strength to carry out what you know is best for you, despite extreme fear, uncertainty, and difficulty. You could experience a lot of suffering at first, but one day you'll wake up and find yourself happy than you could have ever imagined. You'll look back on that day and wonder why you didn't have the guts to act sooner in the 'correct' direction.

Because of this, almost everyone who endures severe misfortune will inform you that what seem to be your worst life experiences are really your greatest benefits.

One of the most challenging situations you will ever encounter is being married to someone who has either borderline or narcissistic personality disorder. It is so challenging since there is no treatment or solution for it. I hope this book has helped you get some understanding of the true nature of the issues and their potential remedies.

Seekers of Punishment

You will get quite familiar with this behavior if you are in a relationship with a narcissist.

Even if you really apologize, you will still need to be punished. Unless they express and believe it to be enough, nothing is ever enough. They seem to believe that if someone is not punished, they will not learn their lesson.

Thus, the relationship as a whole gradually devolves into a power struggle. The narcissistic person adopts strategies for engaging with you that will always put you at a disadvantage.

It becomes commonplace to get rude comments, insults, and criticism for everything you do or say.

You're going to end up constantly saying sorry and being in some way incorrect.

Only you will always have fond memories of the past.

When you could do no wrong in their eyes and received endless sweet words.

Usually, this is the reason you continue.

I'm waiting for those moments to come back.

They get irate when unfavorable things happen to them or when anything obviously shows that they made a mistake. angry with the world in general and the person who started the expose.

Since they are faultless in their own views and never make errors, they are never held accountable for wrongdoing. Even if they are guilty, they believe it is unacceptable for society or anybody to treat them that way. Additionally, they won't stop until they are satisfied with the situation's resolution. This implies that every trick in the book will be used, including finding whatever kind of assistance they can get for themselves. up to the point of need.

When you interact with a narcissist, there is no such thing as a level playing field. Furthermore, neither party is subject to the same set of norms. There is always a clear set of rules for you, generally the ones governed by society at large, but there are no rules when it comes to them.

They are never held accountable for anything, and they are free to act whatever they like.

Because of this, it is best to avoid conflict with one of these individuals, regardless of how correct you are.

They are also like a dog with a bone in that they never let it go on top of all of this. not until they are certain that they have triumphed.

Not even close to being accurate would be to call them vindictive.

They could assume that rage is the only emotion that can influence any circumstance as a result. This kind of behavior is all that many developing youngsters ever witness. People get upset and use their anger to intimidate and dominate others.

The opposing person is threatened, and as a result, cowers in terror and gives in.

Since they were raised with this as a default belief, it stands to reason that as adults, they would also employ rage as a tool to coerce compliance.

This is why it is crucial to spend more time conversing with youngsters as they grow older. should let them know both how their behavior makes you feel as an adult and how dissatisfied you are with it.

We never simply become irascible; there is always a cause for our anger. Education is necessary for those who are learning. They need to be made aware of how their actions impact other people and why it enrages them.

Empathy is a skill that develops once you can begin to picture how you might feel if someone else had done the same thing to you.

when we abstain from torturing, inflicting damage onto others.

Many claim that the narcissistic person suffers from a severe lack of empathy.

Children who grow up knowing that adults are upset with them just because they disobeyed instructions or did not do as they were told will eventually grow up to be the same kind of adults.

They consistently hold the opinion that they ought to be followed without hesitation. that a person in a position of power is always correct and has the upper hand. Sadly, we are the ones that brought about many of the issues we face today.

You are going through a difficult time if you are interacting with a narcissistic person. Every time anything occurs to disturb you, you will have to convey to them how you feel, and then you must hope that a penny will drop somewhere.

In order to maintain peace, you cannot afford to apologize without justification, yet you also cannot remain silent for three days. They will just keep acting that way if you do any of them. pushing you to submit out of rage and administering punishment as they see appropriate.

This may still occur, but at least when you choose to speak out, you will have presented a convincing defense for your position.

How To Handle Narcissists And Prevent Their Negative Effects On You

It's unhealthy to be in a relationship with a narcissist. They may be complex, sensitive, and very self-confident, but that doesn't mean they can't be influenced or won over.

I've detailed dealing with a narcissist in more detail below than simply theoretically. The following are helpful tips that may be used while interacting with narcissistic people. Because they can be verbally and emotionally abusive, they also serve as indicators of when it's time to move on.

1. View people as they really are. Those with narcissistic behavior are excellent at turning on the charm when they want to. Additionally, you can discover that you are emotionally tied to their claims and promises. Additionally, they could only be seen as stylish in professional situations.

Take a close look at how they treat others while they are on stage, however, before you get emotionally involved or dragged into that moment. Don't believe them when they say that lying, demeaning others, or manipulating others won't affect you; it most certainly will!

Don't simply believe what they say or do since it doesn't matter to them; what matters to them is how they'll use you in the end. Therefore, disregard everything they say or do. Don't be duped; trust what you see on stage instead of wondering whether they will change or concluding that it is simply a coincidence! The first step to coping with and avoiding them is accepting them for who they are. You can't really change their mindset, either.

2. Don't pay them any attention and break the spell. People with narcissistic attitudes constantly go above and beyond to keep themselves in the

limelight, whether that attention is bad or beneficial. If you're not cautious, you can end yourself accepting their strategies. You'll unknowingly be putting your needs aside in order to fulfill others.

Although you may have the false impression that you will soon be free of their attention-seeking conduct and be able to endure it for the first time, this will never happen. No matter how much time you spend changing your way of life to accommodate them, it will never be enough. What can be done, though?

Don't let them undermine your self-confidence. Don't let them define who you are or what you stand for; those things make up who you are. You did matter, and when you tell yourself that often, it serves as a reminder that you should be taken into account regardless of what other people say or do.

You may do this by reminding yourself of your qualities, objectives, and preferences. So take control. Always remind yourself that you have a right to have "me time" and that it is never your obligation to repair them.

3. Take a Stand for Yourself. With a narcissist, stepping away from certain situations and ignoring them may be the best course of action, but this doesn't always have to be the case. You will almost always need to speak out.

You must take the settings into account. Speaking out with a supervisor will be different than doing so with your spouse, your parents, your coworkers, or even your friends. You must thus think about and consider the environment.

If you see that someone with a narcissistic personality enjoys using people, try not to show your irritation because if you do, you will just be feeding their conceit and pride. You must maintain boundaries if the time you spend with this person isn't substantial and you don't want to be close to him for a long time.

But you must speak out if this is someone you want to maintain in your inner group. But always go about it softly and quietly. You must demonstrate to them how their actions and words affect your life. And be direct and explicit about how you want to be treated rather than avoiding the topic. And be prepared for the possibility that they won't concur.

4. Draw Explicit Boundaries. You are aware that a narcissist likes being engrossed in themselves. So, as I previously said, circumstances certainly important, but how do you set the boundary?
They don't even notice the limits you have established for yourself if they are attempting to intrude on your personal space or life. You must also establish limits, which is more crucial.

You may calmly inform your coworker that you can manage it and that you don't want him or her to intrude if they persistently eavesdrop on your conversations or call someone you were speaking with on the phone. Don't stop there; also mention the repercussions.

As an example, you can reply that it wouldn't be fair to ignore him the next time he does it. You'd be shocked to learn that they won't disregard your decision. That marks the limit. If it's your supervisor, keep any communication you have inside the boundaries of the workplace. You may even inform them that you won't feel at ease talking about that issue and deny him the opportunity to continue. Thank him formally and go.

5. Be prepared for resistance. Do you believe that a person who mistakenly believes they want to hurt your ego but you end up accomplishing it would be delighted about it and not retaliate? That won't take place. So, be prepared.

They could arrive with their demand is one of the things you should be prepared for. Don't give in; it's simply a play for pity. They could even come back and try to make you feel bad or like you are being unreasonable and controlling. But be prepared to uphold your choice when such times arrive. The next time you attempt that, people won't take you seriously if you don't maintain it.

6. Keep in mind that you are not at fault. A narcissist won't want to accept responsibility if they damage you. Consider how your partner could try to shift responsibility and place the blame on you if it comes from them.

You can be pressured to maintain the peace before taking the fall. You don't need to judge or degrade yourself, however. Instead, maintain your position based on the knowledge of the truth and do not ignore it. Don't simply let someone steal your knowledge of the truth.

Tell him that's not true and attempt to point out where his responsibility rests if he arrives late for an occasion and tries to place the blame on you. Be brave and speak out. Don't conceal the truth once you are 100 percent certain of it. Speak out and be perceptive to observe every circumstance so you may see where injustices are occurring and mistakes are accumulating.

7. Purchase a Support System. Most of the time, the best way to avoid a narcissist might vary depending on the circumstance. Reducing your connection to a coworker will be different from your spouse's or a parent's bond to their kid. But what can you do if your spouse is a narcissist and you're having trouble?

Build a network of nice and modest individuals to help you in your good interactions. If you don't, you can get very depleted. So, if there is an old buddy that you value much, may you attempt to get in touch with them and try to renew your friendship?

Also, start fresh ones that won't put you in danger of getting into a relationship with a narcissist. Spend more time with your family. Additionally, you might enroll in courses if you wish to widen your social circle. Don't be hesitant to get involved if there is any charitable work that may be done in your neighborhood. Take part in activities that will help you meet new people and feel at ease. You get emotional relief, a confidence boost, and more delight as a result of this.

To maintain a successful relationship, both individuals must listen to each other and make an effort to understand one another, accept responsibility for their own shortcomings, and feel that they can have fun in public.

8. Focus on taking immediate action rather than lingering on promises. You are well aware that narcissists often break their commitments. They will pledge to do the things you desire but

won't say they would do the things you despise. Additionally, they often make improvements.

The pledge is really a means to a goal, even if it may seem sincere. Once they achieve their goals, their drive will disappear, making it impossible for you to reconcile their statements with their actions.

The best course of action in this situation is for you to maintain your ground, demand what you need, and then act on it. Maintain your stance that you will only grant their want if they also consider yours. Be constant, since this will enable you to maintain your position and resist caving to their pressure methods. Before you realize it, you have reached your point of need.

9. Consider That He Might Need Professional Assistance. People with narcissistic problems may be reluctant to seek professional assistance because they don't see an issue.

Researchers have also looked at the possibility that narcissists may potentially have another condition. Mental illness or a personality issue may be included. And this may be a cause to get assistance.

You may perhaps be so nice as to suggest that they seek expert assistance. But keep in mind that you can't make them do it. Instead, you must acknowledge that they are in charge of it. Although the narcissistic feature is a mental illness, this does not make harmful conduct acceptable.

10. Determine Your Own Need for Assistance. If you often interact with a narcissist, it may have an impact on your mental and physical health. Therefore, if you suspect that your partner is a narcissist, you may require assistance. However, how would you know if you need assistance?

If you exhibit signs of anxiety or despair and you are unable to describe a specific health condition. Go visit a doctor right now. Following your examination, you can be sent to support groups and other services like therapy. Invite your loved ones and close friends to join your support network. You don't have to handle anything by yourself.

Section 4:
Various Narcissists

The overt narcissist, the open egomaniac who commands you to comply with their requests and display admiration, is the simplest to identify and flee from. It's much simpler to leave such people—who are often narcissistic in an abusive way—once you see the first indications of abuse directed at you. It becomes more difficult if the person in question happens to be your boss or another person in a position of authority, and you have to make difficult decisions in order to get rid of them. Otherwise, it's difficult to ignore how egotistical such a person is and avoid falling into 'romantic' traps with them. It's also simpler for others to identify openly narcissistic individuals since they often burst into narcissistic wrath.

The closet or stealth narcissist, which is the reverse of the overt narcissist, is a very hazardous personality type. Such a person has subtlety, cunning, and they are even capable of executing their own NPD tricks and tactics fairly intelligently. Such behavior often exhibits passive-aggression as a clear sign. This kind of individual works behind the scenes to identify and take advantage of their target. Such narcissists often have highly enticing and ostensibly attractive/pleasant face characteristics and attitudes, which may easily deceive others. Gaslighting, indoctrination, seduction, and other nefarious means of control are all used by covert narcissism, which is a particularly cancerous type of the disorder. In terms of charisma, such a person may be magnetic and captivating; they can covertly entice their victims into a state of bondage that is often romantic or sensual. Their weapons have a facade of beauty and even compassion, but their objective is the other's emotional connection and reliance. Such a person may expose "their true face" by using overt manipulation, emotional blackmail, triangles, jealousy drama, and other techniques once the "bond" has been created and the other has been seduced by the narcissist's attractiveness. However, at that stage the other person is generally very taken with the narcissist, making it challenging to separate and flee even in the face of obvious evil and danger. The ideal target of such a narcissist is often someone who exhibits codependent or masochistic characteristics clearly.

The inverted narcissist is likewise quite cunning and secretive, but unlike the previous scenario, their manipulation does not include as much scheming and a craving for domination. Such narcissists are often highly insecure in a very obvious manner, but they are also incredibly self-absorbed and constantly sing "poor me" songs. Their narcissism suggests that they are unable to recognize each other's needs and desires. Instead, they lack confidence and are self-centered. The inverted narcissist continuously seeks validation from a scenario in which they play the lead role because they are filled with self-doubt. The other person serves as a simple ego extension, which is a well-known function. Such a narcissist is driven by a blatant inferiority problem. They need to compensate for their incompetence/unattractiveness by involving people in ongoing drama because they feel incompetent for a variety of reasons (which are often obvious in their life). They have a mental script that compels them to constantly victimize themselves and wallow in their shortcomings and failings. Naturally, they are unwilling to correct their shortcomings in order to become better. Their desire for drama, greed, and reassurance are what shape their mind. Such a person may sometimes be the ideal codependent since they enjoy the support of a stronger, "real narcissist." The abuse they want will also probably continue to be given to them by that sort of narcissist.

There are some narcissists that are highly brilliant and skilled in some areas of their life. However, since they employ their brains to draw in prey and food, their thoughts may be diabolical. A intellectual narcissist is someone who seldom verbally demands things or expresses narcissistic wrath. The verbal social manipulation methods used by the cerebral narcissist are many and varied. When they hear other people's tales, this person is completely aware of how to manipulate narratives and turn the conversation around themselves in order to obtain social dominance. The intellectual narcissist is skilled at arguing, an adept at setting the tone in practically any discussion, and able to mentally influence the worldviews of others via language and interpersonal understanding. The intellectual narcissist is likewise very dependent on being correct and winning battles. Such a debate master is difficult to defeat. Remember, however, that there are by no means any Socrates, since their motivations are not those of learning, purely logical thinking, or discovery, but rather the urge to maintain their superiority and satisfy their ego via others.

In order to manipulate others and maintain a desirable self-image, other narcissists have propensity to use their bodies and sexuality. Their urge to diversify their pool of sexual partners and admirers is at the heart of their narcissism. Such a narcissist is not content with abstract adulation and is more than likely a true nymphoman or sexomancer. For this person to feel superior, they must always have sex partners available. However, rather than being the result of other talents, accomplishments, or endowments, their prowess seems to be built on a number of partners. Since they exploit sexuality and carnality to fuel their egos, one may describe this kind of narcissist as somatic or erotic. However, remember that their need is not exclusively erotic. Additionally, they are quite exhibitionistic and like boasting about how many partners they have. Instead of being passionate about sex or wanting to get to know someone sexually, their desire is more driven by their ego.

Many other narcissists are accomplished individuals. Although they are successful, their motivation is compensating. It's obvious that their motivation comes from a deeper psychological foundation that also suggests a need for dominance, rather than from a love of their work or a need for money. They use their prosperity and notoriety as narcissistic sources of power and influence. Since they are achievers in some manner (often monetarily), this kind of person is also referred to as the elite narcissist. Finding a narcissist whose ambition and megalomania go hand in hand is the key to reading them. They create a false sense of self to maintain their ego along with riches and social influence. This kind of narcissist often targets those who would make excellent prizes. Such a guy is unlikely to pursue partnerships with codependent, frail women. He will instead target people who are equally wealthy and accomplished, younger ladies, or really top models. The best must be everything that he has! His significance and all-around excellence will be shown through their partners and assets.

If narcissism is coupled with psychopathic characteristics, for instance, it may assume even more hazardous forms. What sets it different from simple psychopathy? Such a person is not motivated by a desire for violence and destruction. If such a person steals or gets raped, their motivation is psychological. An example of a psychopathic narcissist is someone who may commit fraud just to maintain their appearance of being affluent in front of others. As you can see, their motivation is neither exclusively homicidal or materialistic. Fraud is solely used as a means of maintaining the person's supporters and desired self-image. It goes without saying that this kind of narcissism may be violent and even include murder.

Don't Try To Change Narcissists While Dealing With Them.

It is the basic guideline for dealing with egomaniacs. They are convinced that they are typically right, they have no concept of their own fundamental limits, and they are unable to consider the viewpoints of others. They'll often use feelings of guilt, indignation, fear, and weakness to subdue you. Make a mental coercion connection explicit. There will never be an adjustment made to them. Therefore, attempting to compete with them and wasting energy ineffectively is foolish. You must look for yourself if you want to coexist with an egomaniac. And alter your outlook on them so you can tolerate them. The harsh truth in this situation is that trying to change someone else will only make things worse for you. Starting with something simple will have a big influence on how you see what is occurring. For instance, you may think of your interactions with the conceited person as a way to train your mind to use caution, tolerance, and overall focus. Since listening to egotists at work can be so draining, this is a fantastic chance to advance yourself.

Choose Freedom

Hyper-controlling egomaniacs use a variety of tactics to maintain your obedience. They affect your sense of responsibility or gratitude and make you feel guilty. Anything that would make you agree with them. Consider your options and decide how to react without their input while accepting their disapproval or fury. In the unlikely event that someone else overwhelms you, you sell out yourself. Choose the chance that is both a right and a responsibility then. You would forfeit your own character if you gave it up. Nobody can have a good life while adhering to someone else's morals. By choosing opportunity, you may live stress-free for the rest of your life. It is hard to continue debating with a narcissist even when you are correct because they do not want to lose. In this regard, you are ready to proceed.

Keep Your Expectations Low Passive-forceful egotists are ambiguous and nuanced; they often postpone obligations and break promises. They seem friendly yet don't behave like friends. They don't look at problems straight on. They demonstrate their intent by being inert, that is, by never assisting others. They are quite depressing. How do I react? You should not make many assumptions. You'll feel less irritated the less dependent you are on them. By doing this, you will control reality while disapproving of their dishonest behavior. You need to learn how to accept people for who they are. Keep in mind the main principle: they'll never change! When you are managing someone like this, having high expectations of them just makes you more likely to be dissatisfied. Realizing that people often put themselves first and others second is a necessary part of realistically analyzing what is taking place. Since they will almost always put themselves first, you shouldn't make many, if any, assumptions about them.

Avoid focusing on their justifications
It is never a weakness of theirs. If you try to criticize them, know that it will only have a boomerang effect. You will be held accountable for the remarks you make to them.

In terms of thinking, narcissists are not very constrained and have a They need to feel remarkable in this situation so they won't realize they were mistaken. You'll never be able to show them the opposite. So, disregard their "reasons" and continue on your own course. Get used to running things without their blessing. Being incorrect is never an option for them, and they will expend a lot of effort trying to prove that they are correct.

Don't Guard Them
It is often possible for them to share information about your worries with others. They should always maintain a perfect image. They want to continue treating you presumptuously while you remain silent. Particularly with two or three connections, it occurs. They have no right to judge how much of your life

you should give to another person. By continuing to protect the egomaniacs by following their rules rather than yours, you will just put off your despair. Would you choose to experience constant misery? I believe not. You will continue to suffer alone if you can keep them safe.

Be Decisive and Firm in Your Choices

Narcissists typically try to manipulate you by using your sense of duty. They take use of their capacity for empathy and compassion, two emotions they are unfamiliar with. Then, with strong conviction, you should change your empathetic predisposition to protect yourself. The objections of egotists should not assume control over your choices. You must use your mental clarity and true self-preservation instincts. Continue with your decision since they will surely try to dominate you and make you feel sorry.

Utilize assertive rage

Egotists always stir up controversy. It is off-base to allow oneself to be overwhelmed by outrage, yet in addition to curb this is on the grounds that it is stored in a crease of the character and harms it is causing despondency, uneasiness, hatred, pessimism, self-assurance ... A positive method for communicating outrage is confidence all things considered. We protect our beliefs in this way while also recognizing others. Put away hostility, talk solidly and stay steady with the choice taken. Thusly, outrage will be utilized usefully to encourage you, without expecting anything consequently from narcissists.

Stop Justifying Your Choices

Once you have settled on your choice appearance that you are unyielding, try not to legitimize your decisions. Confronted with the obstinacy of egotists, who might want to keep on controlling you, the debate would never end. Moreover, the individuals who give themselves a lot to legitimize their decisions recommend the possibility of not being so certain and of having the option to change choice if there should arise an occurrence of demand. An egomaniac won't ever allow you to win, so your defense doesn't make any difference to them. Try not to fall into this trap!

Be Humble, Don't Become Like Them. Egoism Generates Selfishness.

If you are managing egotists, be mindful so as not to allow yourself to be adapted with the end result of becoming like them. We as a whole have an inborn egotistical inclination and the gamble is to begin treating the egomaniac in an impolite manner. Now the intuition of self-protection becomes egotistical. To stay away from this, we want to zero in on modesty. Without a doubt, the people who are legitimately unassuming are mentally sure and don't have to take more time to their side. He would rather not be tyrannical towards others, and yet doesn't permit others to be against him. Selfishness may gradually turn you int a narcissist!

When you are unassuming you can handle yourself and try not to become like them.

Forgive

The positive parts of absolution are complex. It makes you allowed to zero in on a larger number of significant needs than outrage. It urges you not to get fixated by the individuals who violated you any longer. It permits you to plan ahead. You have no control over the ways of behaving and decisions of someone else, yet with pardoning you can figure out how to acknowledge and endure egotists for what they are. All the more thus, absolution provides you with a true serenity which is very important

www.ingramcontent.com/pod-product-compliance
Lightning Source LLC
Chambersburg PA
CBHW050244120526
44590CB00016B/2215